CATHAL O'NEILL'S DUBLIN

Over its long history G & T Crampton, founded in 1879, has earned a strong reputation for its high-quality construction and development work. Among Dublin's celebrated Crampton buildings the following are featured in this volume: UCD, Earlsfort Terrace, the Berkeley Library, TCD and the United States Embassy. G & T Crampton continue to be a major force in Ireland's construction industry.

The author and publishers acknowledge with gratitude the financial support of G & T Crampton in the publication of
CATHAL O'NEILL'S DUBLIN.

First published in 1998 by Marino Books,
an imprint of Mercier Press
16 Hume Street Dublin 2
Tel: (01) 661-5299; Fax: (01) 661-8583
e.mail: books@marino.ie

Trade enquiries to CMD Distribution
55A Spruce Avenue
Stillorgan Industrial Park
Blackrock County Dublin
Tel: (01) 294 2556
Fax: (01) 294 2564

Published in the US and Canada by the Irish American Book Company, 6309 Monarch Park Place, Niwot, Colorado, 80503
Tel: (303) 530-1352, (800) 452-7115
Fax: (303) 530-4488, (800) 401-9705

ISBN 1 86023 064 4
10 9 8 7 6 5 4 3 2 1

A CIP record for this title is available from the British Library

Cover design by Penhouse Design
Originated by Ikonics

Printed in Ireland by BetaPrint, Unit 2A,
Newtown Industrial Estate, Clonshaugh, Dublin 17

CATHAL O'NEILL'S DUBLIN

Cathal O'Neill

To Deirdre

CONTENTS

'Architecture is the real battle ground of the spirit. Architecture wrote the history of the epochs and gave them their names. Architecture depends on its time. It is the crystallization of its inner structure, the slow unfolding of its form.'

MIES VAN DER ROHE — CHICAGO 1950

INTRODUCTION

I was born in Capel Street, Dublin in 1930 and, apart from five years spent in Chicago in the late 1950s, I have lived all my life in Dublin. From our home in Capel Street, in an early-eighteenth-century townhouse, I could see the City Hall, Green Street Court House, the Debtors' Prison and Halston Street Church. I was within a short walk of the City Markets and the wide spaces of Smithfield and, to the north, Dominick Street and Henrietta Street leading to the King's Inns.

In 1937 we moved to a new home on Griffith Avenue in the suburb of Glasnevin. I can still vividly remember my first visit to the house some weeks before we moved in. The interior was empty of furniture, but it was filled with early spring sunshine and the smell of new wood. The house faced onto the broad boulevard of Griffith Avenue and at the rear a long garden led into farmland which extended uninterrupted to Santry Avenue. Our move to the suburbs brought me into contact with the special delights of the Botanic Gardens, the Phoenix Park and the landscape and buildings of north County Dublin.

My first school, Scoil Colmcille, part of the Model Schools, was in Marlborough Street. My walk to school brought me along Parnell Street, past the palatial Williams & Woods building, the Rotunda Hospital and the Parnell Monument to the Pro-Cathedral, allowing a sideways glimpse at the General Post Office before arriving at the grounds of the school, which had been laid out in the spacious gardens of Tyrone House.

I am not sure to what extent my contact at an early age with so many imposing buildings influenced my decision to become an architect and whether it affected my appreciation of the buildings. What does strike me, however, when I revisit my favourite places, is the simplicity and plainness they share.

After completing primary school at Marlborough Street, I advanced to secondary school at Coláiste Mhuire in Parnell Square half a kilometre away, so my knowledge of the city was extended. My trip to school, by bicycle, now took me past Mountjoy Square, St George's Church and North Great George's Street before reaching Parnell Square. Coláiste Mhuire was located in a terrace of fine mid-eighteenth-century houses and had as its immediate neighbour the wonderful townhouse of Lord Charlemont, which had been converted to serve as the Hugh Lane Municipal Gallery of Modern Art.

At that stage of my life I had never thought of Dublin as exceptional. I had never been abroad and assumed that Dublin was smaller but similar to most other cities. As Dubliners, we were outwardly proud but secretly suspicious of the many claims made on our city's behalf: that it was the second city of the Empire, that O'Connell Street was the widest street in Europe and that the Phoenix Park was the largest park contained within any city in the world.

I began a new relationship with the city when I entered the School of Architecture at University College Dublin. The location of the university in Earlsfort Terrace, Newman House and the College of Science in Merrion Street brought me into contact with a whole new section of the city. Meanwhile, the lectures from Professor McDermot in the theory and history of architecture explained the basic rules of composition and were illustrated with reference to the buildings and cities of the world. We drew and painted buildings and practised our technique on visits to the more important monuments. Our summer vacations were spent hitch-hiking in Europe, and each return to Dublin brought the scale and quality – along with the shortcomings – of our city into context.

The third and final phase of my relationship with Dublin

began on my return to the city in the early 1960s with my wife Deirdre and our two children, having spent five years in Chicago. This was the time of the so-called post-war boom, which, in terms of construction, seemed to be confined to office development in Ballsbridge and the indiscriminate expansion of housing in the suburbs. There was a feeling of optimism, however, and some good new buildings to justify it. In particular, the two universities, Trinity College and University College Dublin, promoted architectural competitions which resulted in a number of modern buildings of outstanding quality, including the Berkeley Library in TCD and the Administration and Arts faculty building in UCD.

In the thirty years since then, amid controversy and compromise, inaction and reaction, the city has been substantially restored, consolidated and reinstated. Many different interests will claim responsibility for this success, but the irresistible attraction of Dublin and the vibrancy of the people probably played a key part in its development.

The illustrations in this book were painted on location or in some cases were sketched on site and completed in the studio. In addition, photographs were taken as a guide to the accuracy of the details. The drawings were made on Ardèche watercolour paper and are on average twice the size of the published work. Most of the illustrations were done in summer, as evidenced by green foliage, bright skies and sharp shadows cast on the façades, which help define the form of the building and display the details.

Drawing a building 'from life' can be an enlightening exercise, because you can reconstruct a building stage by stage, piece by piece, and at each stage of the drawing you can pause and consider the appearance of the building in its incomplete state. You can ponder on the quality of the Custom House without its dome, for example, or think about whether No. 85 St Stephen's Green was improved by the later addition of No. 86. Making a sketch of a building helps to reveal the subtlety of the design and the skill of the architect.

The purpose of the book is to share with others the pleasure of growing up in Dublin and the appreciation of some of its buildings and landscapes. In any collection of work the selection is influenced by personal taste, and in this case the choice is emphatically personal. My own taste, circumstances, experiences and haphazard encounters with some buildings more than others led to their inclusion. Many buildings, especially from the last quarter of the century, for which I have great admiration but limited experience or understanding of have been omitted.

I hope this book will encourage people to look more closely at buildings, old and new, and try and discover why they like or dislike them. Maybe then, in time, we may become more discerning in our taste and continue to build into the next century with as much style and confidence as we have had in the past.

PART ONE

At School and Play

A VIEW OF DUBLIN

The two arm-lengths of land culminating in Howth Head to the north and Dalkey Hill to the south seem to welcome visitors to Dublin in a warm embrace. There is something especially exciting about sailing into Dublin Bay from far out at sea in a westerly wind and any kind of a swell. As you tack towards the land the outline of the gentle hills comes into view and then quite suddenly, while you are still a distance of several kilometres offshore, the wind drops, the sea is calm and the air warms as if the city had changed the weather for your personal benefit. The sunshine might even break through for a moment and catch the sharp spires and the green domes. Then the view of the city disappears again, blocked by Howth Head, as you steer north between the head and Ireland's Eye towards the safety of Howth Harbour with the golden sliver of Portmarnock beyond.

Dublin Bay is a safe enough haven although its many sandbars are a danger to larger ships. It must have been irresistible, nonetheless, to the first visitors who came here and sailed up the Liffey to establish the town. From Howth Hill there is a clear view of the city and the southern suburbs as far as Dalkey Hill and its tiny island. In the background is a silhouette of the Dublin Mountains and to the left are the Sugarloaf and Wicklow mountains and Wicklow Head.

The cliff walk from which this sketch was made extends from Howth Harbour above the sea cliff to Sutton, a distance of eight kilometres. As children we spent many happy days there swimming in the disused seawater swimming pool of the Jameson family; we could cool our sunburn on the journey home on the top of the open-topped tram. This cliff walk and its southern counterpart on Dalkey Hill are two of Dublin's most valuable resources.

CLANBRASSIL STREET

My mother was born in Clanbrassil Street in 1896. The house is a substantial two-storey redbrick residence typical of the early- and mid-nineteenth-century housing development which followed the transport lines of the tram and railway. It has a deep plan with a double A roof which, together with its large, well-proportioned windows, creates the impression of a Georgian townhouse. My mother often recalled happy childhood days strolling along the banks of the nearby Grand Canal, measuring the distance walked in terms of the number of locks passed.

In his novel *Ulysses*, James Joyce chose Clanbrassil Street as the birthplace for the hero Leopold Bloom. This was not surprising as the large Jewish population in Dublin in the late nineteenth century lived in the area. Shortly before her death in 1991, I brought my mother to her old home in Clanbrassil Street and showed her the plaque on the nearby house which states:

Here in Joyce's imagination
was born in May 1886
Leopold Bloom
citizen, husband, father, wanderer
reincarnation of Ulysses

Astonished, she could not come to terms with the fact that a plaque had been erected to commemorate the imagined birth of an imagined man in a real house. Like many Dublin people of her age she had a love–hate relationship with Joyce and *Ulysses*. When Richard Strick's film of the novel was first screened on the television my mother watched it and afterwards phoned me to criticise its obscenity. 'It was so bad,' she said, 'I turned it off three times.'

THE MODEL SCHOOLS, MARLBOROUGH STREET

My first school was Scoil Colmcille, which was the all-Irish section of the Model Schools in Marlborough Street. I was taught by a remarkable couple, the O'Sheas. Mrs O'Shea was a musician; upon hearing my voice, she banished me to the room furthest from the singing class where I was given paper and pencils and left to amuse myself. Seamus O'Shea was a skilled artist and encouraged all his pupils to draw and model with plasticine. He had a collection of beautiful polished wooden shapes, cubes, spheres and cones and he made compositions with the pieces, allowing us to observe them for a few minutes; then he would dismantle them and test our ability to reassemble them to match the original. He also taught us to play football. The schoolyard was divided into squares, two players per box. The grid made for disciplined football and later in life proved useful in architecture.

The classrooms were demolished in the 1970s but the entrance block from Marlborough Street still stands and has been recently renovated. Built in the middle of the nineteenth century, the building has a certain military severity and intimidating scale but it works well as a school. Large windows facing east and west give excellent even lighting to the classrooms and good cross-ventilation. The high ceilings are generous in proportion and are environmentally sound.

PORTMARNOCK STRAND

Portmarnock Strand is twelve kilometres from the city centre and is Dublin's most beautiful beach. The Velvet Strand, as it is appropriately called, is four kilometres long, safe, clean and made of the finest cream-coloured sand imaginable. The beach is sheltered from the prevailing wind by cosy, grass-lined dunes and on the seaward side is punctuated by two islands, Lambay and Ireland's Eye, to form what is almost a bay. The most important aspect of Portmarnock Strand is the sense of openness. Sand, sea and sky form one vast expanse. Indeed, it is hard to believe that such an unspoiled place can be so close to a capital city.

From the 1920s my parents rented a small cottage near the first green of Portmarnock golf course. The family moved there for the summer and my father commuted from the city on his motorbike. I am told that I was present at the take-off of the *Southern Cross* from the beach in 1930. The plane, piloted by Charles Kingford Smith and a crew of three, landed in Newfoundland thirty-one hours later and went on to become the first plane to circumnavigate the world. There is a photograph in the family collection of my parents with a baby in arms – presumably me – posing in front of the plane. The *Southern Cross* was a heavier and larger plane than the *Bremen*, which flew from Baldonnel airport on the inaugural east–west flight in 1928. Portmarnock Beach was used for the take-off of the *Southern Cross* because of the length of the beach and the firmness of the sand and also, I like to think, to give the airmen an immediate sense of freedom.

TYRONE HOUSE

I passed through this gate every day on my way to school with my sisters Sheila and Cassie and my brother Paul yet I cannot say that I remember anything of it. Designed by Cassels in 1740 for Lord Earlsfort, it was later acquired by the Department of Education and in the late nineteenth century a replica was built further north on Marlborough Street to provide matching entrance pavilions to the group of buildings containing a number of schools.

When I revisit the building now I realise how plain and dour the façade is and how intimidating it must have been for a six-year-old. It faces west so that in the morning it is always in shadow and the grey granite walls add to the severity. I am struck by its simple plainness; it is devoid of ornamentation and seems to anticipate the shape of things to come in the form of early-twentieth-century architecture – the houses of Adolf Loos, for example.

Here the heavy cornice forms the window sill of the upper windows so that the top floor is like a modern penthouse and the coping on the parapet above suggests the edge of a concrete flat roof!

THE PRO-CATHEDRAL

I passed by or through this building every day on my way to the nearby school in Marlborough Street which probably explains my lifelong attraction to the Greek Doric order. I suppose I was in awe at the scale and power of the building which even today seems too large for the site.

A new space in scale with the building could be created if the garden of the Department of Education were made public, the boundary railings and perhaps the trees removed and the street pedestrianised. I have omitted the railings and gates of the church from my sketch as I think they emphasise the large bulk of the building on the restricted site. The design of the Pro-Cathedral in 1820 is clearly derived from the Temple of Athena and Hephaistos, a much smaller and well-preserved temple in Athens built from 449BC to 444BC. It is not known for certain who the architect of the Pro-Cathedral was as it was built as a result of an architectural competition and the drawings were unsigned, but it is widely believed to be John Sweetman.

In the early 1980s I was commissioned by Archbishop Ryan and the administrator Father Paddy Dowling to redesign the sanctuary to conform to the new liturgical regulations. During research for the project we discovered an unsigned drawing which, although undated, would appear from the dress of the congregation to be contemporary with the opening of the building. It showed a spacious open sanctuary with a delicate altar rail. In the new design the railings and the balustrade between the columns around the sanctuary have been omitted and a new altar, the focal point of the liturgy, has been placed on a floor of Portland stone directly under the centre of the apsidal semi-dome.

GRIFFITH AVENUE

Griffith Avenue was built between 1926 and 1928 within a few years of the establishment of the Irish Free State. This remarkable boulevard, which extends for a distance of four kilometres from Fairview through Drumcondra to Glasnevin, was a wonderfully ambitious project and was intended as a model for road building in the new state. City architect Horace O'Rourke was responsible for the design which was known as the 'hundred foot road' until 1927 when it was renamed after Arthur Griffith. There are two continuous rows of plane trees in wide grass verges on either side of the avenue. The comfortable semi-detached houses have generous front gardens and the overall distance between houses is forty-five metres. The perspective created by the four lines of trees and the gentle curve closing the vista gives Griffith Avenue its distinctive quality. Despite the popularity of the road with the general public the design was unfortunately not repeated elsewhere. Although the houses on nearby Collins Avenue are broadly similar to those on Griffith Avenue, Collins Avenue is much narrower and has only a single row of trees on each side. The contrast between the two spaces demonstrates most forcibly the value of scale and landscape.

I moved with my family in 1937 to a new house on Griffith Avenue. One of the most vivid memories of my childhood is my first sight of the avenue, the white concrete paths and road, the pale green grass verges, the new foliage and the seemingly never-ending perspective. As children, we learned to cycle, skate and play football on Griffith Avenue, as there were few cars to trouble us before or during the war. We were frequently troubled by the guards, however, who would swoop on us from side streets and capture us where we played.

'And what is your name and address?'

'Frank Duff, 14 Mobhi Road'

'Can you identify yourself?' asks the guard as he writes in his notebook.

'Yes,' replies my friend Frank, producing from his pocket a photo of himself taken at his First Holy Communion.

The guard looks repeatedly to and fro between Frank and the photograph saying, 'Aye, that's you all right,' and departs satisfied.

It was on Griffith Avenue that I saw my first traffic lights, reputed to be the first lights installed outside the city centre. They were placed at the junction of the avenue with the main Dublin–Belfast road. We walked the mile down to see this great invention; the lights were not timed then but controlled by rubber pads placed on the roadway. We hid behind the trees and waited until we saw an approaching car, whereupon we would jump on the rubber pads to turn the lights red against the driver.

LINZELL HOUSE

Linzell House provided my first encounter with modern architecture. It was a few hundred yards from my house on a lane connecting Mobhi Road and Ballymun Road. The house was designed by the English architect Harold Greenwood in 1928 and built by Robert Linzell, a successful English housebuilder. It is reputed to be the first concrete house in Ireland. In Linzell's time it seemed as impenetrable as a castle, with high walls to the lane and a well-protected large rear garden to the south. Later, it was sold to an Irish family with two sons of our age, and so we came to know the house from the inside. The plan is L-shaped around the entrance court and its cascading fountain reminded us of the Californian mansions we had seen in films.

Revisiting the house now brings a sense of disappointment. The Central Fisheries Board uses the house for offices, and its desks and filing cabinets make it difficult to imagine the rooms being lived in. The layout is rigid with no hint yet of an open plan and, apart from the continuous arcade along the south side, there is little connection between the interior and the garden. Yet the house has a definite impact reinforced by the unexpected shape of the elevation and the telling use of horizontal bands. These bands greatly increase the apparent length of the building and have the technical advantage of improving the weathering quality of the smooth plaster.

THE MANSION HOUSE

To most people of my generation the term Mansion House did not refer to the elegant town villa located at the top of Dawson Street but to a large circular room with a conical slate roof which is located directly behind the Lord Mayor's House. It was in this room and the adjacent smaller rooms that we appeared from the age of about seven in countless performances of poetry, recitation, storytelling, Irish dancing and drama as part of the annual Feis or Arts Festival competitions.

The Mansion House is one of the oldest houses in Dublin. It was built in the early 1700s by a Mr Dawson and purchased about 1715 by the city as the Lord Mayor's House. Originally it had a simple brick elevation, but it was gradually altered in the nineteenth century to its present appearance. The rendered and painted façade and its setting back from the street on what appears to be a generous site give it a distinctive and rather country air. As with other Dublin buildings a wrought-iron and glass canopy was added in the 1890s to protect the dignitaries making the short journey from their carriage to the hall door. The introduction of these protective roofs in Dublin and elsewhere coincided more or less with the popular use of the umbrella.

Sensitive improvements were carried out in 1991 to mark the occasion of Dublin City of Culture, including the reinstatement of the cobbles and bollards to the forecourt and the restoration of the Oak Room.

HOUSES ON HOWTH ROAD

At the end of the war I often went with my parents to view houses for sale. I am not sure whether they were seriously interested in moving or whether, in common with many other young couples then and now, they found it a pleasant pastime. One of my most memorable viewings was our visit to the newly constructed semi-detached modern houses on the Howth Road designed by the architects Robinson, Keefe and Devane. The houses are located about halfway between Raheny and the seafront. The main feature of the plan was the projection of the staircase forward of the housefront in a semi-circular tower with a tall narrow window. The unusual position of the stairs freed up the rest of the plan and gave it a spacious, open feeling. There was a hardwood floor throughout the ground level which, together with the bright sun shining through the large south-facing windows and the absence of curtains or furniture – showhouses were unfurnished in those days – evoked for me a feeling of freedom and exhilaration.

The exterior of the house was even more remarkable. There was no roof, at least not one that could be seen, and there was no decoration; even the curved canopy seemed to be functional, sheltering people as they made their way around to their waiting car. A certain prominence was given to the garage and that reflected the growing importance of car ownership. Today the houses are still attractive and are much sought after. They are in good condition and generally have not been interfered with except in some cases where the original steel windows, which gave the houses a certain scale, have been replaced with plastic frames and large sheets of glass.

BULL ISLAND BRIDGE

Bull Island was created as a result of the construction in Dublin Bay of the Bull Wall, which caused a change to the pattern of tides. The resultant silting added to the existing sandbanks to form what is now the 460-acre island. Until 1975, when a new embankment was put in place, the only access to Bull Island was across a narrow wooden bridge. As children we often cycled there to swim from Dollymount Strand or the Bull Wall. We always walked across the bridge because the space between the planks was exactly the width of a bicycle tyre, which made cycling hazardous. On sunny days it was a pleasure to walk barefoot on the warm boardwalk and feel the texture of wood grain and sand underfoot.

DUBLIN AIRPORT

I still remember the excitement of my first visit to Dublin Airport in 1940. I was a boy scout and our scoutmaster believed that field trips to buildings new and old should be part of our education. We listened with pride as the guide explained the technical innovations of the building, which had not yet opened for business: the special diffused lighting which we were told did not cast shadows, the secret heating panels in the walls and ceilings which overcame the need for ugly radiators and the patented flat roof which was guaranteed not to leak. But the brightness and expanse of the interiors were what really fed the imagination. There was a sense of being inside a full-scale model of the future.

In later years I was to discover how well the building accommodated the excitement and pleasure of air travel. Arriving by car at the entrance, one was immediately struck by a sense of modern opulence as sunlit surfaces and bright interiors took the place of the glittering decor of an earlier age. From the large two-storey central concourse and booking hall the space led easily to the departure lounge on the left and the arrivals and customs areas on the right. The simple circulation on one level has not been matched in any modern airport except perhaps London's Stansted. A generous lounge–dining-room with a designated dance-floor on the first floor afforded a panoramic view of the airfield. External balconies extended the length of the building and gave it a ship-like quality. From here relatives and friends could cheer departing honeymooners or welcome returning emigrants. Of course the relatively small scale of the operation gave the whole process an intimacy which would not be possible today, but there was vision and understanding of social interaction in the design.

The building, designed by a team of architects from the Office of Public Works lead by Desmond Fitzgerald, has many of the elements of the new modern architecture – plain plastered surfaces, horizontal strip windows, large glazed curtain walls and glass blocks housing the stair towers – yet the symmetry around a central axis is surprising and is clearly in deference to the earlier academic tradition.

Dublin Airport was a daring and courageous building for its time and place and might have sparked a vigorous modern movement in architecture in Ireland but for the advent of the war, after which opportunity and confidence waned and did not re-emerge for more than thirty years.

THE PHOENIX MONUMENT

Having learned our football on Griffith Avenue we quickly graduated to proper pitches with goalposts in an area of the Phoenix Park known as the 'Fifteen Acres'. Due to the concentration of the playing fields a type of impromptu football fair took place every Saturday and Sunday at the Gough Monument – now demolished – and the Phoenix Monument. We would go there with our boots and togs and, to be absolutely sure of a game, a ball, and wait around to be chosen by one of the self-appointed team captains.

The Phoenix Monument was commissioned by Lord Rothwell and built in 1784. In our time it was opposite the gates to Áras an Uachtaráin, where it stood like a milestone or a viewing stand halfway along the broad boulevard. It is now restored to its original location in a roundabout in the centre of the main road, apparently serving as a traffic calming device. It seems somehow less effective but the elegance of the design remains. A simple plinth in the shape of a four-leaf clover is surmounted by a flight of steps leading to the engraved base and slender column on which stands the delicately carved image of the phoenix.

The precision and beauty of the design was brought home to me when making this sketch, as an error in the position of the column almost ruined the composition.

Beautiful objects demand careful handling.

THE DOG POND, PHOENIX PARK

We grew up believing that Dublin was in some respects the world's greatest city. We were told it had the biggest city park anywhere and this boast was not too far from the truth. The Phoenix Park spans almost 2,000 acres in area, making it larger than the Bois de Boulogne or several of London's parks put together. Although the park consists mostly of open parkland and sports fields it has also a number of intriguing small-scale spaces.

The Dog Pond, more properly called the Citadel Pond, is one of these. Located south of the main road about a kilometre from the Parkgate Street entrance, it is a circular pool situated within a grove of evergreen oaks. The water is overshadowed and dark and the breeze that funnels under the trees makes it a cold place. Despite its eeriness, we were attracted as children to what seemed a foreign landscape in an Irish park. Near the end of the war a crater was formed when a bomb was dropped beside the pond. It was about the same size as the pond and the two together produced a curious, even surreal combination; two holes in the ground, one full, one empty.

When I returned there for the first time in many years I was disappointed at the neglected air of the place. The pond was overgrown, the railings partly demolished and the trees no longer formed a neat circle.

In the background of the sketch is a hazy image of the Wellington Monument built in 1815 to the design of Robert Smirke. This grand obelisk, standing at sixty metres tall, serves as a useful reference as it can be seen from many parts of the city. It was the tallest structure in the city until the construction of the Electricity Supply Board's twin chimneys.

THE MAGAZINE FORT

On Thursday afternoons we went from school to the Phoenix Park to practise football and hurling for the coming weekend matches. The bus dropped us at Islandbridge Gate and we walked from there the short distance to the sports field past the Magazine Fort. The fort was built in the early eighteenth century and still serves the military. It had a threatening air; the blank walls with only slits for windows peered out disapprovingly at all who passed. At times it took on the appearance of a submarine in a sea of grass. This impression was enhanced while we walked towards it up the steep embankment for it seemed to rise higher and higher until its full height was revealed standing in the dry moat that surrounds it. We would often kick the ball to one another as we made our way to the football pitch and occasionally the ball would land in the moat. Then there was an argument as to whether the kicker or the errant fielder should retrieve it. It was with some trepidation that the ball was retrieved because there was always a fear that something untoward would happen down in the moat.

Many years later I heard the story that during the Rising in 1916 a group of Irish volunteers and Fianna Éireann played a football match close to the Magazine Fort during which the ball was kicked over the wall. The players gained entry to retrieve the ball and capture the fort.

CHARLEMONT HOUSE

The fortuitous location of my school, Coláiste Mhuire, next door to the Hugh Lane Municipal Gallery of Modern Art, formerly Charlemont House, gave me and my friends a priceless opportunity to experience modern art early in our lives. At that time school trips were unusual and I do not recall any formal visits there, although a number of us frequented the gallery throughout our time in secondary school. Curiously, my memories are less to do with the paintings than the spaces, whose brightness and continuity were a revelation as each room lead intriguingly into the next. I assumed the building had been designed as a gallery, and it was not until later that I learned that it had been the townhouse of Lord Charlemont and was designed by Sir William Chambers in 1746. Although its interior had been substantially altered when it was converted to a gallery, the façade is virtually intact. The beauty of the building lies in the way the architect has set the building back from the street behind the line of the adjoining houses, forming a forecourt with the curved screen walls obscuring the awkward corner connection. The setback reinforces the importance of the building and creates a strong axis with the public garden opposite.

At some point in my visits to the gallery I became aware of the blank walls of the innermost gallery, on which were placed miniature reproductions of the Hugh Lane Collection with a cryptic explanation that these paintings rightly belong to the Irish nation, and had been so bequeathed by the late Sir Hugh Lane, but were now in the possession of the National Gallery of London. I do not remember being particularly offended by this, but it would have reinforced the strongly nationalist ethos of my schooling. Consequently, we were all delighted when some years later Paul Hogan, a student at the College of Art, audaciously removed one of the paintings from the collection of the National Gallery of London, having forewarned the newspapers that a significant event would take place at the entrance to the gallery on that day. His action undoubtedly led to the agreement whereby the collection is shared between the two cities.

For most young boys, visits to art galleries were considered sissyish or voyeuristic or both, so we had to slip into the gallery in the hope of not being noticed. Visiting the gallery was a case of choosing your moment and your friends.

THE BOTANIC GARDENS

The glasshouses in the Botanic Gardens known as the curvilinear range are surely among the most delightful buildings in all of Dublin.

The demand for large glasshouses was stimulated in the nineteenth century by the new interest in the growth and propagation of exotic plants from warmer climates. The challenge was to make an enclosure with the maximum sun penetration and the least obstruction from the supporting structure.

The design by James Turner in 1843 combines an intuitive sense of engineering, a mastery of metalwork, an understanding of passive solar energy and an inspired visual sense. Lightness is achieved by the use of slim wrought-iron mullions which run from the granite base to the lantern light which appears to hover above the roof although is in fact supported on slender columns. To increase transparency even the pilasters have panes of glass inserted in their centre. Only the gutters disguised as an architrave are opaque.

The size and profile of the cast-iron mullions, which are only 25mm thick and 300mm apart, are designed to provide the maximum structural ability with the minimum obstruction. The line of the mullion is vertical as far as the gutter and then it continues in a complex curve which is steep at first and gradually flattens out towards the centre. This particular shape has the advantage of elongating the vertical section of the structure and reducing the span of the inclined portion. In addition, the shape of the curve resists wind-loading and reduces the chance of snow lodging on the roof. More significantly the curved surface of the glass is more or less at right angles to the rays of the sun during the day, thus ensuring maximum solar gain within the glasshouse.

The range deteriorated over the years and was at one time in danger of demolition, but in 1997 the Office of Public Works undertook a complete and faithful restoration and when the new plants have matured the beauty of this space will be complete.

When we were young we spent a lot of time in the Botanics. The hothouses with their exotic plants and equally exotic girls from the local Holy Faith Convent made it an attractive place to be after school or even during school hours during those cold winters of the 1940s.

CROKE PARK

Croke Park is the headquarters of the Gaelic Athletic Association, founded in 1884 to promote football, hurling, camogie and handball. The new stadium, designed by Desmond McMahon and his partners, is the first part of a plan to encircle the entire pitch with a stand to accommodate 80,000 spectators. It is an exciting new design in which the heavy concrete base of tiered seating, weighed down as it were by spectators, is contrasted with a light steel structure which floats above like the wings of a hang-glider. The apparent weightlessness of this large canopy is achieved by suspending it from the steel supports which are concealed above.

Croke Park is hallowed ground for political and sporting reasons. It was here on 21 November 1920, on Bloody Sunday, that British troops invaded the ground during a game and shot at players and spectators, killing twelve people, including one player. All important matches are held here and it is the ambition of every young follower of gaelic games to play on the sacred turf.

Coláiste Mhuire, where I was a student, was an enthusiastic but not very successful participant in inter-school competitions. Once we reached the semi-finals of a minor competition against the favourites, O'Connell's Schools. We had so few students that everybody got an opportunity to play. I was chosen as a substitute even though I had one arm in plaster from an earlier injury. At least I was sure of being part of the team photograph in that historic arena.

In 1918 my father established a sports manufacturing business and every year since then the company has supplied the football known as O'Neill's All-Ireland for all important matches.

THE GPO

Only twenty-five years separate the opening of James Gandon's Custom House and Francis Johnston's design for the General Post Office, yet the change in architectural taste in such a short time is remarkable. Appropriately, Johnston replaced Gandon as the country's leading architect and designed other important Dublin buildings, including St George's Church and the Chapel Royal.

The GPO is a distinctly nineteenth-century building which relies for its effect on a simple shape expertly arranged in perfect proportions. The building gives some idea of how effective the slightly larger portico of the Pro-Cathedral would have been if it had been located on O'Connell Street as originally planned. The somewhat simplified illustration does not quite capture the sense of *gravitas* which this building has for me.

My school had a republican ethos and we frequently visited the GPO to read the Proclamation of the Irish Republic beside the entrance door and admire the polished black marble of the Cúchulainn statue.

I remember the building serving as an impressive backdrop to military parades and political gatherings after the war, but now it seems indignant at the loss of Nelson's Pillar and the handsome order of the street.

THE O'CONNELL MONUMENT

All the statues in O'Connell Street look across the River Liffey to the southside of the city, perhaps with longing. As a youngster growing up on the northside I seldom had occasion to cross the river so that the statues, particularly this one on the boundary between the two halves of the city, were inevitably seen in silhouette. The grey-green pattern of the bronze seems suspended in mid-air, supported on the pale limestone base. The elevation of O'Connell above the masses perfectly captures his position in history. The seated angels lounge comfortably on the base watching the life of the city with expressions of wry amusement.

The structure was designed as a result of a competition won by John Henry Foley and took nineteen years between 1864 and 1883 to complete. The base with Éire Casting off her Fetters and the winged figures was done by Thomas Brock.

I have a special place in my heart for Daniel O'Connell, to whom I owe my one real success at an interview. Asked whether I could deal with confrontation, given my perceived mild manner, I quoted the story of O'Connell's assistant who took over the brief in the High Court when his senior was called away unexpectedly. Arguing the case on the prepared brief he came upon a note in the margin, 'Argument weak, raise voice.'

THE HA'PENNY BRIDGE

This is probably the first modern construction in Dublin. Built in 1816 as a toll bridge, this fretwork of cast iron spans the width of the river as effortlessly and delicately as a spider's web. Its shape expresses the structural function without adornment. The low curve of the bridge is like that formed by a stone skimming the water and provides a convenient gradient for pedestrians as well as sufficient headroom for the Guinness barges that plied the river. The apparent lightness is achieved by the elegant structural design of the arched ribs which support the walkway. The tapered profile of the structure, deep at the quay walls and shallow at the centre of the span, accurately reflects the forces acting on the bridge and achieves the engineering ideal of maximum effect with minimum effort. The arches are constructed from cast-iron pieces which are cruciform in profile. Their projecting ribs cast fine shadows which emphasise the sinuous shape of the bridge.

It is generally agreed that the bridge was made at Coalbrookdale in Shropshire, the site of the first iron bridge built in 1791 – a potent symbol of the Industrial Revolution. It is not known for certain who designed the Ha'penny Bridge but my colleague Seán de Courcy, Professor of Engineering, recognises the hand of Telford, one of the greatest bridge-builders in history.

The toll bridge was built to replace an existing ferry and the charge of a halfpenny for each crossing was continued until 1916. I must have crossed the bridge many times but my only memory is that of a blustering wind and a fear of the bridge collapsing.

PART TWO
College Days

NEWMAN HOUSE

The first introduction for many students at University College Dublin to this group of buildings, known collectively as Newman House, was at the matriculation examination held every summer in the redbrick Aula Maxima, the building on the extreme left. Those successful in the matriculation returned to the university for their first term the following October. Students spent much of their spare time at No. 86 St Stephen's Green, the largest building of the group. It had a student canteen at basement level, common rooms on the hall floor and meeting rooms on the upper floors. We came here for lunch from Earlsfort Terrace and in the evening attended college society meetings, self-consciously re-enacting the precocious performances of James Joyce and his colleagues, who were students there from 1898 to 1902.

No. 86, reputedly the work of the architect Robert West, was built by Richard Whaley in 1765 while he was living in the smaller adjoining house. The design demonstrates the versatility of the eighteenth-century townhouse plan. A central entrance and staircase serve a number of rooms on each of the floors so that the building was well suited to its original role as a family house, with a strong emphasis on entertainment, and subsequently to its role as the foundation building for the university. Later still, when the university moved to new premises in Earlsfort Terrace, it served equally well as a students' union. The façade is a grand version of a typical Dublin townhouse built in stone. The importance of the first floor is emphasised by taller windows with alternating pediments above. The size of the upper windows is reduced to reflect the lesser functions of the upper floors.

The adjoining two-storey house, No. 85, was built in 1738 to the design, it is thought, of Richard Cassel. It is more obviously a family house; its plan is dominated by a magnificent staircase running at right angles to the main axis and leading to the superb first-floor salon which extends the entire width of the house and overlooks St Stephen's Green. The façade of No. 85 is more self-contained than that of No. 86; indeed, it seems to be unaware of its neighbours. The central triple window emphasises the importance of this main room and subdivides the space into three zones, a useful device in eighteenth-century entertainment.

University Church, which was built in 1865 in the rear garden of an earlier redbrick townhouse, marks its presence by means of an elongated porch which reaches out to meet the street. The design of the building is based on Byzantine images and uses *trompe l'oeil* combined with marble mosaic and gold leaf to simulate the interior of an eastern church.

IVEAGH GARDENS

If St Stephen's Green was the public park for students at University College Dublin then Iveagh Gardens was their private garden. The gardens fill the block south of the Green between Harcourt Street and Earlsfort Terrace and connect the premises of the university at Newman House to those at Earlsfort Terrace. It is a secret place, largely unknown to the public, and in our day it was a favourite haunt for lovesick students. During Trinity term it was a popular place for study. The students, often in pairs, would lie on the shade-speckled grass and try to concentrate on their subject.

The landscape is Italianesque. Weathered plastered statues from the 1865 Dublin Exhibition confirm the geometry of the gravel paths bordering the lawns. One section contains a sunken lawn that was originally used for archery but in our time was the perfect pitch for many inter-class football matches, in particular, the annual staff-student match.

The history of the gardens is complex. At one time they were known as Leeson's Fields and subsequently became the gardens for Clonmel House, which was on the west side of Harcourt Street. In 1817 the park was made public and renamed Cobourt Gardens. The gardens were later acquired as part of the 1865 Exhibition and the design in which they were laid out is to a large degree the one that exists today. The Office of Public Works is planning to renew the gardens and make them more accessible to the public.

UCD, EARLSFORT TERRACE

UCD's front building, facing onto Earlsfort Terrace, was built between 1912 and 1918 as a result of an architectural competition won by Rudolph M. Butler, who later became the Professor of Architecture. This was the main centre for University College Dublin until it moved to the new campus in Belfield in 1962. The severe neo-classic design with its plain heavy details and hard grey limestone gives the building a somewhat dour and unfriendly tone. Nonetheless, most graduates have happy memories of their time there and especially of the main hall, now the concourse of the excellent National Concert Hall designed by Michael O'Doherty of the Office of Public Works. It was the space around which all activity revolved when we were students there, from our first day, when we stood in awe at the sophistication of the older students and met other youngsters who would become our lifelong friends, until our last day, when the results of our final examination were read from the steps of the grand staircase by J. P. McHale, the College Secretary.

BUSARAS

Busaras was the first large modern building of the International Style in the city. The design by Michael Scott was begun in 1944 but due to political wrangling the building did not open until 1953. The relative merits of Busaras and the Airport Terminal were the subject of much debate during our student days. There was the question of which style would prosper, the more restrained, European-style airport or the brash bus station based on the American skyscraper; there was also the question of which building would remain functional into the second half of the century.

The building is composed of three elements; two rectangular blocks of differing heights are joined at the ground floor by a curved glass screen and overhanging roof. It is an exciting composition full of interest and interplay between the different surfaces, and there is humour in the restrained use of Italian mosaics to signal three special functions: the diagonal blue stripes of the bus controller's room, the circular red columns of the ministerial suite and the striped canopies of the staff restaurant on the penthouse.

Most Dubliners have never been in the building and view it only as an irritating backdrop to their magnificent Custom House. The building is worth a visit and is best enjoyed by approaching it like our country cousins on a provincial bus, which brings passengers first through the building and then in a gentle curve around the concourse before coming to a stop under the remarkable canopy.

THE SHELBOURNE HOTEL

Despite its height and bulk, the Shelbourne Hotel fits comfortably into the varied scale and architecture of St Stephen's Green. John Curdy designed the building in the 1850s and used a number of architectural tricks to good effect. Projecting mouldings and plaster panels, for example, make for an appealing light-hearted façade, and the two large bay windows serve to reduce the apparent length of the building. The detail of the bays with their tall, narrow brick piers is designed to combine the ground and first floors into what appears to be a single storey. A similar device is used to join the second and third floors, which are separated from the next floor by a white plaster band. The top floor is cut off from the rest of the elevation by the projecting cornice. The overall effect gives the impression that the six-storey building is perhaps only three or four storeys high. The use of white painted plaster in the panels and around the windows reduces the area of brick and imparts a gay, festive appearance, reflecting the contribution the Shelbourne has made to the city for over a hundred years.

For students in nearby Earlsfort Terrace, the Shelbourne was the most convenient and elegant establishment for refreshments, although it was way beyond our means. One of the senior students was a regular customer and therefore assumed to be wealthy until we joined him one day for coffee in the lounge. When the bill was presented he put his hand down between the seat and the back of the couch and found enough coins to pay the bill.

THE NATIONAL LIBRARY

A confluence of three disciplines – literature, art and politics – occurs at the precise point where the entrance steps of the National Library almost touch the railings separating it from Dáil Éireann. Behind the library, the National College of Art had its rather cramped premises and to reach it students had to pass through the narrow gap with one leg shorter than the other. This restriction seems to intensify the importance of this small area of hallowed ground which over the years every important writer, artist, and politician passed.

As part of our course in architecture we spent two afternoons a week in the College of Art learning to draw from life and the antique. It was generally a rewarding experience except when our teachers, including Sean Keating, resignedly took our pencils and with a dazzling display of technique captured the subject precisely. I realised then that good teaching is more about encouraging the pupil than a display of skill by the teacher.

The National Library was designed by Sir Thomas Deane in 1885-90 and forms a pair with the National Museum, which is on the opposite side of the forecourt. The diverse functions of the library and museum are cleverly accommodated in similar forms, and the recent cleaning and restoration of the façades reveals the subtle contrast between the warm colour of the sandstone colonnade on the ground floor and the darker tones of the granite blockwork in the drum and the upper structure.

MOUNT STREET

Mount Street connects Merrion Square and the Grand Canal via a short diversion around St Stephen's Church, which stands firmly in the middle of the crescent. The street is not as grand as its neighbours; the houses are smaller, less varied and the south-facing façade (left-hand) is built from what appears to be inferior yellowish-brown stockbrick.

A typical red brick is used on the opposite side of the street where the houses are more elaborate with granite facing to the ground floor. But the details of the façades are less important than the overall effect of the street, as is true elsewhere in Dublin. Here all the attention is on the perfectly proportioned St Stephen's Church on which all the lines of the composition – parapet, windows and railings – converge.

St Stephen's is sometimes used for concerts as well as for church services. Its simple interior has excellent acoustics and in the summer the pleasure of the music can be followed by a stroll along the banks of the canal.

MARSH'S LIBRARY

Marsh's Library, the oldest public library in Dublin, was designed in 1701 by William Robinson. The attraction of this building lies in the simplicity of its façade. The elevation, with its symmetrical layout and steeply pitched roof, has a childlike quality. The very large windows on the first floor, which represent almost fifty per cent of the wall surface, reflect the fact that this is where the books are stored and read. The rhythm created by the four windows and the pairs of stone corbels projecting from under the gutter adds interest without being fussy. The supporting corbels occur over the solid portions of the wall, emphasising the simple construction and logic that lie behind the design.

The rear elevation which opens onto a delightful garden is less satisfactory. The overhanging roof and the large brick piers between the windows appear to belong to the mid-nineteenth-century restoration.

THE RUTLAND MEMORIAL

Built in the late 1790s as a public drinking fountain, this beautiful object in Merrion Square West is a favourite measured drawing subject for architectural students. The gently curved screened wall and the subtle contrast between the granite blocks and the white Portland stone of the string-course ensure that it is always fun to paint.

In this case, the generosity of the donor ensured that something with a purely utilitarian purpose became a beautiful object. It is easy to imagine the water carriers seated in the niche waiting their turn to collect fresh water from the fountains while enjoying the sense of permanence and civic pride which emanates from the monument.

The iron railings have been omitted from the sketch as presumably they were absent from the original and they obscure the delicate lines of the composition.

MOFFET HOUSE

I recall cycling to Portmarnock as a young student to see two new houses designed in the 1940s by Noel Moffet. Noel was an avant-garde architect, a town planner and a member of the White Stag Group, which promoted modern art. He moved to England after the war and contributed regularly to architectural journals there. The houses are set on a ridge of high ground on a large site against a fine stand of mature trees. The plan is simple with entry from the north and all rooms facing south. The elevations are plain but with subtle inventions which set them apart from their contemporaries. For example, instead of the ubiquitous flat roof, a low pitched roof with a single slope is used and allowed to overhang the south-facing wall, suggesting a need for shade and a more exotic climate than exists in Portmarnock. The right-hand gable projects forward on the façade as if to protect the windows from the east gales blowing in from the sea. The need for functional vents in each bedroom is used to create a decorative motif with concrete discs which punctuate the elevation.

Originally the two houses stood as a pair alone in open parkland; now they are almost obliterated by a dense new housing development. Clearly the promise of a new architecture has not been fulfilled.

THE RETORT BUILDING

As the name implies this was a condensation chamber for collecting vapours produced in the manufacture of coke by the Dublin Gas Company. Located between the south quays and Grand Canal Street, it was the most striking modern building on the Dublin skyline until it was demolished in the late 1980s.

Although the structure was designed by a British firm of engineers it bore a superficial resemblance to the sketches of the Italian Futurists of 1914 who proposed images for the city of the future. The use of exposed structural steel, plain smooth brick and glass block panels in a grid-like pattern was even closer in appearance to the work of Mies van der Rohe in Chicago in the late 1940s and fitted his description of earlier work as 'skin and bone architecture'. When the building became redundant in the 1970s, the School of Architecture in University College Dublin with the help of the Dublin Gas Company conducted a project proposing new uses for the building. The alterations necessary to get sufficient light into the building, however, were such that the existing balance of the composition would have been destroyed.

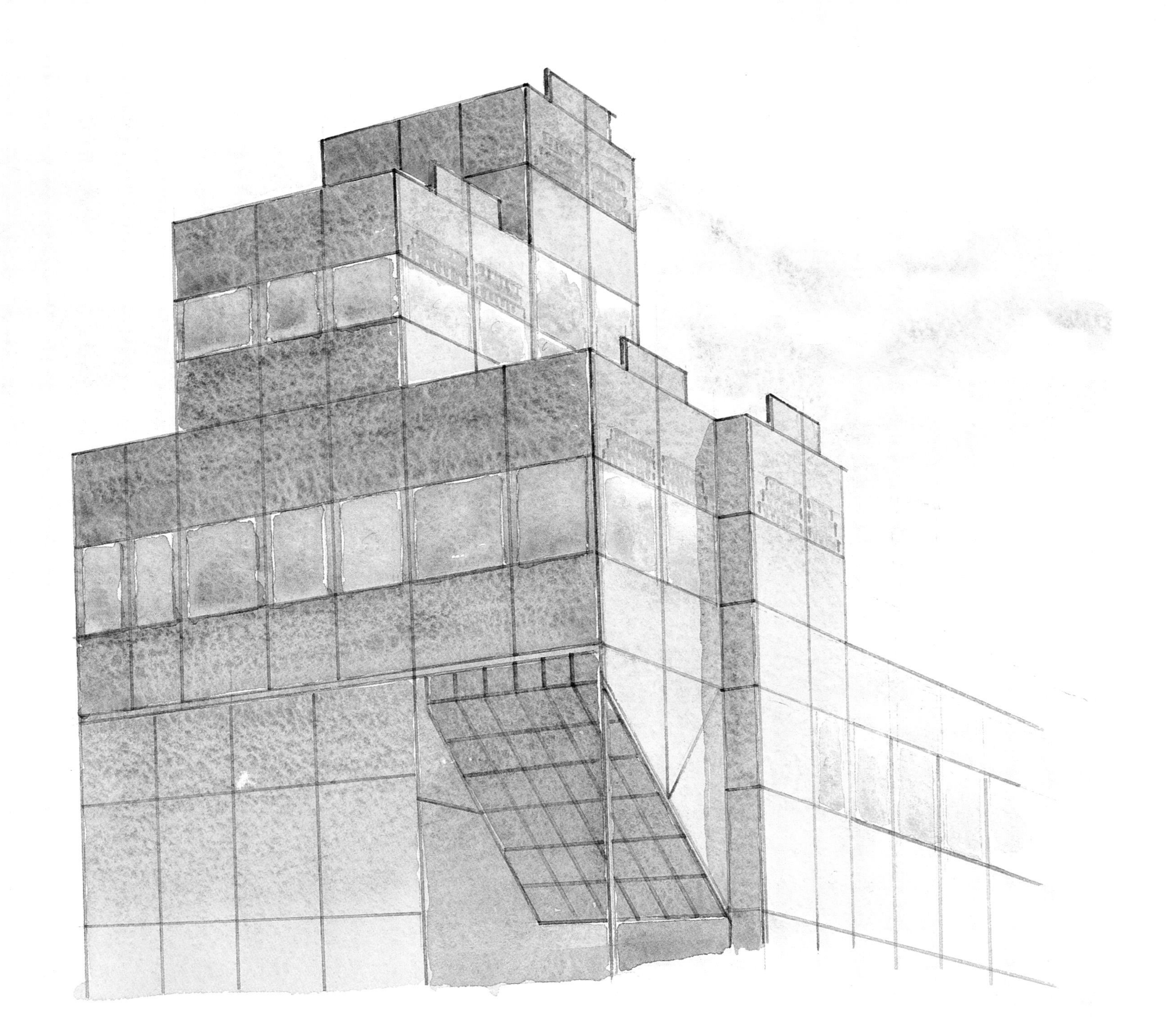

THE TWIN TOWERS

The Joyce Tower and Michael Scott's nearby house, 'Geragh,' can be seen as twin beacons guiding the arrival of modern literature and architecture to Ireland.

James Joyce spent a brief holiday in the Martello tower and subsequently chose it as the location for the opening chapter in his novel *Ulysses*. Scott acquired the site about 1936 and in the following few years he built his house, which became an important icon for young architects. He acquired the Martello tower in 1962 and it is now the Joyce Museum.

The original sketches for the house suggest a more ambitious project but the built version retains the principal idea of a ship-like building with a rounded end forming circular bay windows with matching balconies. The building consists of two blocks set at thirty degrees to each other. The rear block contains the entrance hall, kitchen, dining-room and children's bedrooms. The front block, which is higher and dominates the composition, contains the living-room, main bedroom above and the garage and store at ground level.

The house makes reference to contemporary European buildings and possibly the curved shapes of the Martello tower and Dublin Airport. Nonetheless, it is an original concept that responds to the shape and character of the site. The contrast between the restricted entry sequence and the open space of the living-room with its panoramic view of the bay is carefully planned and the subtle shift in the form of the curved windows, each different in size and alignment, gives the composition a dynamic quality.

The building marks Michael Scott as an architect of talent and imagination who contributed more than anyone to promoting modern art and architecture in Ireland.

HEUSTON STATION

There are certain similarities between Heuston Railway Station and the original Dublin Airport. Through their high quality of architecture, each adds a certain grandeur to the traveller's arrival and departure.

This building was designed by the English architect Sancton Wood in 1846 as a frontispiece to the existing train hall. The architect imagined it as an impressive gateway to the city through which the public would pass with the least obstruction and the greatest pleasure. But the single small front door suggests that it was never intended for the public. In fact it was used exclusively for the company's directors while the passengers came and went through doors at the sides of the building.

The redevelopment of the station by Iarnród Éireann will open the main entrance to passengers, who will pass through the building to the train hall behind, and the changes will allow a clear view of this calm and elegant elevation.

THE CUSTOM HOUSE

As part of the course in architecture at University College Dublin, we were required, every June, to measure and draw many of Dublin's public buildings. With the aid of ladders and sometimes scaffold supplied by the college we scrambled in teams over the city's monuments and spent much of the summer completing the drawings for submission on the first day of the next term. I have measured many of the buildings illustrated in the book and without doubt the Custom House is the one which gave me the most pleasure.

It is a magnificent building and its scale and prominence are enough to establish Dublin as a European capital city. Viewed across the river, which reflects the creamy Portland stone façade and open arcaded ground floor, it appears positively Venetian – an enlarged Fondaco Dei Tedeschi perhaps. Before the quay wall was raised above the road level and with a high tide it was not difficult to imagine the Liffey lapping the front steps. I sailed up the river before the Matt Talbot Bridge was built and realised what an impressive sight it must have presented to visitors arriving by sea to the city. In his picturesque views of the city, Malton captures this scene with a sketch looking downstream towards the Custom House with large sailing ships at its doorstep in what appears to be a dangerously high flood tide.

What is most satisfying about the main elevation is its poise. The architect James Gandon has arranged the seven distinct parts of the façade like people posing for a formal family photograph. Each is individual yet closely related. The central portico dominates and is flanked by two pavilions which are repeated with variations at both ends while in between are the two long arcaded wings, all overseen by the essential dome – withdrawn and aloof.

A perfect pose, a powerful composition, and yet there is more to it than image. The functional plan is accurately reflected in the elevations. The central and end blocks mark the junctions with the buildings behind and the arcaded sections subtly suggest the two internal courtyards.

Criticism has been levelled at the use of the darker stone in the reconstruction of the drum of the dome after the 1921 fire, but now the upper portion of the building matches the darker grey granite of the sides and north elevation and the white Portland stone is confined to the most important frontage to the river. Thanks to meticulous restoration by David Slattery and the Office of Public Works, this frontage has been returned to its original condition.

The Custom House has been propitious for Dublin in two ways. It set a standard for public building and it brought architect James Gandon to the city, where he lived and practised for the rest of his life.

HARCOURT TERRACE

This is one of the few groups of houses in Dublin that are rendered and painted. It is a virtual cul-de-sac, a backwater at right angles to the Grand Canal. The elegant neo-classical composition is surprisingly successful given that it occurs on only one side of the terrace and looks across at a motley collection of two-storey buildings on the other. The rigid symmetry of the pairs of houses has caused planning and painting problems. The owner of No. 5 is unsure where to draw the line. The house is two windows wide on the upper floors but its yellow paint is carried into the centre of the pediment and then irresistibly into the full niche.

The terrace has had some famous residents and notable events. On this house a plaque states that the world première of George Russell's *Deirdre* took place in the back garden. Sarah Purser had her studio in No. 11 and Míchéal Mac Liammóir and Hilton Edwards lived at No. 4. They gave us invaluable help in our school days with their production of Shakespearean plays which had been chosen for the Intermediate and Leaving Certificate courses, and they continued to educate us in our adulthood with their eclectic taste and bravura acting. Míchéal, the unmatched storyteller, and Hilton, the perfect foil, were equally entertaining off the stage. Shortly after Míchéal was conferred with an honorary degree a friend phoned and asked to speak to Dr Mac Liammóir. 'He is not at home,' replied Hilton. 'Would Nurse Edwards do?'

CHANCERY PLACE FLATS

The flats in Chancery Place are among the many housing schemes built by Dublin Corporation in the 1930s. The building was designed by George Simms and combines a sensible plan with carefully considered elevations. Although this large four-storey building is immediately to the east of The Four Courts it does not compete with or distract from it. The building is reduced in scale by fragmenting the composition into a number of elements expressed in different materials. The three upper floors are rendered and sit on a brick base at the ground floor, and brick is used again in three-storey towers at either end of the building. The refined nature of the design demonstrates how even with a demanding brief and a limited budget a good architect can design a modest building that will enrich the overall fabric of the city.

THE IVEAGH BATHS

This remarkable building on Bride Road near St Patrick's Cathedral is one of the few examples of art nouveau architecture in Dublin. It is part of the large charitable housing development built in 1907 by Lord Iveagh, the proprietor of Guinness. The houses that can be seen on the right-hand side are well built but severely functional in contrast to the free architecture of the baths. Unfortunately the street is too narrow to permit a view which would embrace the entire composition.

When I moved to Chicago in 1957 I encountered many buildings by Frank Lloyd Wright and his contemporaries which bore a striking resemblance to our Dublin gem. The main characteristic of this style is the carefree composition of the disparate parts, five windows of varying size, decorative panels, a dome and an inscription all arranged around the entrance. Its importance is emphasised by the steps breaking through the gap in the stone wall and the deep shadow of the porch.

How wonderful this building would be as a pavilion in a spacious and landscaped site.

NEWCOMEN'S BANK

This is a jewel of a building with the most elegant elevations in Dublin. It is difficult to appreciate the south façade when viewed from the narrow confines of Castle Street but the calm east front of the building shown here faces towards Dame Street with a bemused gaze like that of the Mona Lisa. Originally this elevation was half its present width, but in the 1850s the building was doubled on this side by duplicating the existing elevation and adding the porch. The strength and perfection of Thomas Ivory's designs have survived the enlargement.

Postgraduate students of architecture at University College Dublin have analysed the proportions of the elevations in a search for the magic formula. The design has a strong mathematical basis both in the general layout and the detail. This elevation is described within a circle contained between the plinth and the cornice and between the inner edges of the recessed corners. This can be demonstrated by placing a small circular object on the drawing. When making this sketch I mistakenly omitted the recessed corners and I was puzzled by the squatness of the building. Later I inserted the strong vertical lines in each corner and the building immediately came to life.

Despite Ivory's apparent reliance on mathematics I do not believe he designed to formula. He clearly had a wonderful eye which is evident in every part of this building. I have omitted the neighbouring buildings from this illustration because I always see the bank as an independent object, delicate and transparent in the pale luminous cladding of Portland stone.

What a pleasure to draw such a beautiful object.

PEMBROKE STREET

Many streets in Georgian Dublin provide views of the city which, apart from the traffic, have not greatly changed from the time of the original building. This sense of completeness, continuity and containment is the essential quality of that period. A contributing feature is the curved street or the T-junction which limits the view and extends the expectation of more delights to come.

The view looking south-west on Pembroke Street with Fitzwilliam Square on the left is a good example of this. The street runs straight past the square and then curves to the right to make a perpendicular junction with Leeson Street. The vista is limited and there is no sight of Hatch Street with its Victorian Hatch Hall or the modern office buildings beyond. The view is homogeneously Georgian.

The first building on the left before Fitzwilliam Square demonstrates the usefulness of rebuilding in an earlier style for the benefit of the overall street scheme. The building was designed by Professor Desmond Fitzgerald and built about 1960. Although this façade is too long and uniform to convincingly represent a Georgian terrace, the façade on the square is faithfully restored and the overall scheme succeeds in framing the original spatial concept of the square.

I worked for Professor Fitzgerald during the early stages of this project and recall the difficulty in locating a suitable brick. Colour photographs were dispatched abroad without success and eventually I made a number of watercolour sketches of adjoining façades which were used as a reference in the manufacture of the bricks.

KILMAINHAM GAOL

The present Kilmainham Gaol was built in 1780 on the foundations of an earlier gaol. It fell into disrepair and disuse about 1900 and was unoccupied at the time of the Rising.

The execution yard is a bleak place. It is about the size of a tennis court and is enclosed on all sides with a four-metre high wall made for the most part from calp, a characteristic grey-black Dublin stone. Access to the gravelled courtyard from the gaol is through a low doorway protected with an iron gate and there is a pair of large wooden doors at one end of the space giving access to the street.

It was in this space in May 1916 that the leaders of the Rising against British rule were executed. It is generally agreed that the executions were a turning point which led to the War of Independence, which in turn led some years later to the establishment of the Irish Free State. This cold dark space remains one of the most powerful memorials imaginable to any conflict. Standing alone in this sunless space isolated from today's world it is easy to imagine the events of 1916. The walls are scarred but not from bullets, as a line of sandbags was placed behind the victims.

The events are recorded in a bronze plaque opposite the entrance and at the east end a small cross marks the spot where the first twelve prisoners were shot. At the west end a cross marks the site of James Connolly's death. He was injured in the fighting and on 16 May was brought from hospital by ambulance, carried through the large doors, placed in a chair, blindfolded and shot.

PART THREE

Dublin Rediscovered

THE UNITED STATES EMBASSY

I was living in America when the design for the United States Embassy was published amid much controversy. Its critics held that it was the wrong building in the wrong place. They argued that it was totally un-Irish in appearance and described Ballsbridge as a Dublin slum. In defence of his design, the respected American architect John Johansen claimed that the building actually had strong Irish roots and that the design was based on round towers and ring forts. Dublin critics, however, maintained that it looked more like a stretched Aran Island sweater.

The building has many virtues in urban design terms; it resolves the problem of turning the corner at the junction of Elgin Road and Pembroke Road, and the choice of white concrete and granite is consistent with the Dublin tradition of using stone for monuments and important buildings against a background of redbrick terraces. The elevation combines a most innovative use of pre-cast concrete units to support the floors and roof with large plates of tinted glass held in bronze frames. The building rests on a circular granite plinth – an echo of the ring forts. The plan is simple; the perimeter offices are arranged in a circle on each floor around the central three-storey-high atrium. In the past this atrium was used as an auditorium and was ideal for small groups of performers. In the days when the embassy felt more secure, it stood in a broad plaza dotted with the mature trees preserved from the original garden. Today the building is protected by high railings around the perimeter of the property which detract from the original design and the urban plan.

I only fully appreciated the ingenuity of the shape when I was making this sketch. It is a most difficult building to draw.

BERKELEY LIBRARY, TRINITY COLLEGE DUBLIN

The international competition for the design of the new library in Trinity College in 1961 challenged architects to place a modern building on hallowed ground between two historic buildings, the Thomas Burgh Library built in 1712 and the Deane and Woodwards Museum built in 1858. The brief for the competition restricted the height and plan of the building yet required a large volume of accommodation. Consequently many of the submitted designs took the form of a shoebox. What distinguishes the winning design of Ahrens Burton and Paul Koralek is the way they have manipulated the surfaces of the simple block with such intuitive skill to produce an object so pleasing to the eye that it seems to complement rather than compete with the adjoining buildings.

The pleasure of viewing this building is intensified by observing it while strolling in a broad semi-circle from the mid-point of the museum building across the cricket pitch through the gap at the south end and into the middle of Fellows Square. In this way the dynamic composition of recessed and projecting planes can be fully appreciated. The skilful use of modern materials, including large sheets of curved and tinted glass and exposed concrete columns and beams, together with traditional granite masonry, ensures an entirely comfortable mingling of the new and old buildings. The interior is no less remarkable. The traditional use of the roof for top lighting is extended by making openings in the intermediate floors which allow the daylight to filter down through the building.

My own connection with this building is somewhat peripheral. In the mid 1960s I gave an annual course of lectures on modern architecture in the basement of the building. What a pleasure it was to be able to demonstrate first-hand, by virtue of our presence within this masterpiece, some of the theories of modern architecture.

THE RTÉ ADMINISTRATION BUILDING

This is perhaps the finest office building in Dublin yet is almost unknown to the general public, even though it is located beside the Stillorgan dual carriageway which is used by thousands of commuters every day. Designed by Ronnie Tallon in the late 1960s it is a sympathetic and skilful interpretation of the ideas of Mies van der Rohe. The four-storey building is the vertical element in an otherwise horizontal group of outstanding buildings, all of which were designed by the firm of Scott, Tallon, Walker.

Glass-wall office buildings owe their original design to two disparate sources, the skyscrapers of Louis Sullivan in Chicago at the turn of the century and the proposals for glass office towers by Mies van der Rohe in the 1920s. These ideas reached their ultimate expression in the Seagram office building in New York in the 1950s.

This genre of architecture has been widely copied but seldom understood. In this case, the beauty of the structure depends on the refinement of the composition as the proportion of each part unerringly relates to the whole. The building exudes a calm presence and is equally pleasing from all sides, like a Palladian villa. The glass box floats above the ground as if not wishing to obstruct the views of the landscaped gardens.

This building should serve as a reminder to us all of the importance of restraint in architecture.

CARROLL'S BUILDING

This building is one of a small number built in the early 1960s which gave encouragement to those of us who believed in modern architecture. I was teaching at the time in University College Dublin and on Saturday mornings I brought students from the fourth year on site visits to buildings under construction. Carroll's was memorable for its mixture of simple structural system and complex spatial arrangement.

The building was designed by Paddy Robinson (Jnr.) of Robinson, Keefe and Devane, who sadly became gravely ill during its construction.

There is a happy relationship between the building's two reflective planes; the glass and the canal water. The lines of the canal banks are echoed in the long horizontal shadows under the projecting floor slabs which are uninterrupted by the vertical elements of the staircases and lifts set back from the main façade. This is no speculative building but a carefully crafted construction of Portland stone, plate glass and stainless steel in which the proportions are well judged and the problem of accommodating a warehouse conference centre and an office in one building has been imaginatively handled.

FITZWILLIAM STREET

Stretching a distance of one kilometre, Fitzwilliam Street is the longest Georgian street in the city. It runs in a gentle upward slope from the north-east corner of Merrion Square across Baggot Street through Fitzwilliam Square to Leeson Street. Indeed, it creates the illusion of being even longer as it appears to run all the way to the foothills of the Dublin mountains, a further six kilometres away.

The streetscape is full of incident. The basic element of the design is the standard tall narrow townhouse and this is repeated throughout the length of the street. There are many subtle and accidental variations to the main theme, however. The bricks used in the construction, which were mostly imported as ballast on ships from England, differ in colour and texture from house to house. The parapet line varies with the differing heights of the houses and the irregularity of the chimney stacks. The window pattern is generally similar but does change very slightly in response to the change in floor levels from one house to the next, and the different treatment of the doorways and the occasional addition of balconies add further to the variety. At midday the sun shines almost directly down the street which sparkles with colour and the reflections of the white painted linings to the windows. The streetscape is further enriched by the break in the west-side provided by Merrion and Fitzwilliam squares.

In 1965 the Electricity Supply Board made a controversial decision to replace the terrace of seven houses in Lower Fitzwilliam Street with a modern office building. The winners of the competition, Sam Stephenson and Arthur Gibney, made a brave attempt to capture the rhythm of the street with pre-cast mullions made from brick-coloured concrete. My submission to the competition, which was placed second, proposed a bronze-faced building which sought to complement the patina of the existing façades. Now, thirty-five years later, I wonder whether either proposal was wise.

DR STEEVEN'S HOSPITAL

Designed in 1721 by Thomas Burgh, architect for The Royal Hospital Kilmainham, Dr Steeven's Hospital is one of the least known and most intact spaces in Dublin. It served as a hospital for about 250 years and is now the headquarters for the Eastern Health Board.

The steeply pitched slate roof, the absence of the parapet and the small-paned windows all give the authentic image of an early-eighteenth-century building. The building is simple and functional; the large windows give good cross-ventilation to the wards on the upper level and the open colonnade at ground floor provides for the sheltered exercise of patients. I remember visiting my aunt here in the 1960s and believe that I saw patients convalescing in beds in the open-air arcades.

THE WINDING STAIR BOOKSHOP

No. 40 Lower Ormond Quay was built about 1900 to replace an earlier building destroyed by fire. The new building is somewhat taller and wider than its neighbours and instead of mimicking the style of the typical townhouse the design is based on that of a nineteenth-century warehouse. Large windows fill the front elevation and help light the deep plan. The structure is simply expressed with four broad projecting structural piers attached to the front wall. The deep spandrels between the windows suggest heavy-load-bearing floors.

I have always been attracted to this building. It seemed to me to be so much better in this instance to replace a demolished building with a new building which responded to the needs and the construction of the time rather than build a weak imitation of the past.

In 1985 University College Dublin was invited by Dublin Corporation to prepare a study of the Dublin city quays and the project was undertaken with enthusiasm. We rented the top floor of this building as a site office and studio which served us well during the several months of the project. We concluded that the quays could be revitalised by conserving the important buildings and infilling the derelict sites with new modern buildings. The subsequent redevelopment of the quays is welcome, but a main thoroughfare of a capital city deserves more than the widespread use of mock-Georgian houses.

THE FOUR COURTS

If Gandon's Custom House has a Venetian feeling then his Four Courts is essentially Roman. This is conveyed by the weight of the building, its pale ochre colour in the evening light and above all the use of the Pantheon, that great Roman temple, as a model for the central hall. Whereas the Pantheon is a large domed space lit through a single opening in the roof, Gandon's rotunda is a much more complex creation. It has two domes. The outer dome can be seen from many parts of the city and serves to signal the importance of the building and mark the focal point of the plan, and the inner dome forms the ceiling to the main hall of the courts.

There is a degree of falseness in this design inasmuch as the external appearance does not reflect the internal space. Nevertheless, the massing of the buildings is masterful. The architect had to work with the existing block by Thomas Cooley at the western end of the site. He repeated this design at the eastern end of the building with the entrance block and the dome above in the centre, leaving two deep recessed courtyards opening onto the quays. The design and placement of the two arched screens which connect the three blocks is a stroke of genius. It preserves the continuous line of building along the river front, visually links the plane of the pavilions to the decorative central block and discreetly screens the courtyards and the surrounding offices. The central hall, like its Roman predecessor, is a magnificent space although brighter and more in the scale of humans than gods. It is the anteroom to the Four Courts where the public meet with their lawyers and size up the opposition and conveys a sense of a rehearsal room prior to the real drama.

THE CASINO AT MARINO

Designed about 1769 by William Chambers for Lord Charlemont as a pavilion in the garden of his estate, this building is widely regarded as the most beautiful in Ireland. For me it is an enigma. It has the appearance of a monument or mausoleum where one would expect to find the reliquary contained in a single central space. In fact it has two floors over basement and although there is only one entrance door and three windows visible, the building contains seven rooms and a staircase. The architect's ingenuity is demonstrated by the manner in which one of the windows provides the daylight for the stairs and two rooms on different floors. The selection and assembly of each classical element displays great control and judgement.

The building was derelict for a long period but fortunately was acquired by the state and lovingly restored by the Office of Public Works.

I was familiar with the building from my childhood as it marks the eastern extremity of Griffith Avenue and was a frequent destination for a short cycle or a long walk. In the early 1960s, before it had been renovated, the students from University College Dublin somehow got permission to hold their annual party in the basement and I went along as a young tutor. During the night there was a loud banging on the door. Fearing gatecrashers, Professor Desmond Fitzgerald demanded to know who was there. 'We're from Bolton Street,' (the other School of Architecture much disapproved of by the Professor) came the answer. 'I don't care what street you are from,' he replied. 'You may not come in here.'

GOVERNMENT BUILDINGS

This rather grand design was built in 1912 to serve as the College of Science, which was amalgamated with University College Dublin in 1929. It housed the School of Engineering until 1986, when it was lavishly refurbished to serve as the Government Buildings. The feature of the building is a splendid circular room twelve metres in diameter known as the tower room, which served as a boardroom and staff common room in its college days. It was here during the so-called Gentle Revolution in the spring and summer of 1969 that the staff-student committee of the School of Architecture – the first such committee in the university – met in day-long sessions debating the form of future education in the faculty.

I was a member of the committee, along with two students Liz O'Driscoll (now McManus) and Ruairi Quinn, who, twenty-five years later, met again in that same room as ministers in the government of the Rainbow Coalition.

THE GRAND CANAL

The Grand Canal was built during the second half of the eighteenth century and connects the River Liffey with the Shannon at Shannon Harbour. It was a bold engineering feat and passes through forty-three locks in its journey of eighty miles. Its purpose was to provide transport of goods and people, but its passengers were soon won over to the more efficient railways and the transport of goods effectively stopped at the end of the Second World War. But the Grand Canal and its northern counterpart, the Royal Canal, continue to serve Dublin well. The continuous strip of water and its tree-lined banks cut through the suburbs and mark the natural edge of the city. The whole system is made from many distinct parts, each functional and pleasing to the eye; simple cut-stone bridges, deep stone-lined locks and heavy lock gates with long hand-worn lever arms made from single baulks of timber.

For many years I walked this stretch of the canal every day on my way to work and I thought how lucky any city is that has a canal with trees and water and a poet to celebrate it. Patrick Kavanagh lived around here and caught the spirit of the place exactly. A commemorative seat was erected to him just beyond the lock gate with his poem 'Lines Written on a Seat on the Grand Canal' inscribed on it.

O commemorate me where there is water,
Canal water preferably so stilly
Greeny at the heart of summer. Brother
Commemorate me thus beautifully,
Where by a lock Niagarously roars
The falls for those who sit in the tremendous silence
Of mid-July. No one will speak in prose
Who finds his way to these Parnassian islands.
A swan goes by head low with many apologies,
Fantastic light looks through the eyes of bridges —
and look! a barge comes bringing from Athy
And other far-flung towns mythologies.
O commemorate me with no hero-courageous
Tomb — just a canal-bank seat for the passer-by.

THE EDUCATIONAL BUILDING SOCIETY HEADQUARTERS

The centrepiece of this group of buildings in Westmoreland Street was built in the 1900s for Lafayette the photographer, whose name was engraved on almost every photograph in our family album. At some time in our college careers it was converted to the Paradiso Restaurant which we frequented for its late-night continental atmosphere and inexpensive food. In the early 1970s, Sam Stephenson converted the corner building to new offices for the Educational Building Society, using an elegant version of mirrored glass which was new to Dublin's city centre. The result was successful and demonstrated how a street could benefit from some contrast with the general pattern. The EBS later acquired the centre and left-hand buildings and they were amalgamated with the earlier development.

The overall effect is intriguing. Two different versions of the mirrored glass curtain wall are arranged on either side of the stone centrepiece. Viewed in perspective, especially from the O'Connell Street end, the treatment produces a lively street architecture which benefits from the reflections of the Bank of Ireland.

The design may owe much to the difficult interior planning problems and the piecemeal development of the site but the result is a pleasing and restrained addition to the city.

THE BANK OF IRELAND, FOSTER PLACE

Visitors to Dublin must be puzzled by what appears to be a Roman coliseum in the city centre yet Dubliners accept and even admire the windowless screen wall of the former parliament building, which now houses the Bank of Ireland. Its bulging presence constricts the main north–south thoroughfare between it and the curved railings of Trinity College.

The high wall extends from Westmoreland Street in a broad sweep to Foster Place, interrupted only by the east and west doorways and the main entrance portico. The curved granite wall with its deep niches and attached columns is a handsome structure.

The building brings together the talents of three of Ireland's leading architects. Lovett Pearce was responsible for the original building and its main portico, James Gandon designed the east portico and the extraordinary screen wall and Francis Johnston wisely repeated the blank wall with its lively modelling on the west side leading to Foster Place.

Johnston was also responsible for closing the street to create one of Dublin's most delightful spaces. South-facing and virtually free of traffic, this area is cobbled, sun-filled and secluded behind mature pollarded trees, reminiscent of Paris, complete with laconic taxi drivers.

One day when I was unable to fit a model of a building into my car to bring to a critical meeting with a client, I rushed to the taxi rank and proceeded to measure the boot of each of the waiting taxis to see if any were large enough for the model. As the shirt-sleeved drivers watched with amusement, one called out 'Hey mister, it'll be extra for alterations.'

FITZWILLIAM SQUARE

Dublin Georgian squares are in fact rectangular in shape. Although they are formed with almost identical redbrick terraces, each square is different in scale and spatial quality. The degree to which the squares are open or closed depends on the local street pattern. For example Mountjoy and Merrion Squares have a number of streets entering at each corner but Fitzwilliam Square is formed between two parallel streets, giving a pleasing sense of containment.

This sketch from the north side looking towards Fitzwilliam Street shows the subtle variations of the theme of the standard townhouse. The window heights diminish from the ground to the top floor except for the first level or piano nobile which is higher to reflect the increase in the scale and importance of these rooms. In places the ground floor has been faced in stone and occasionally wrought-iron balconies have been added. The houses are different in height and floor levels, giving a lively ripple to the elevations. The front wall of the house is carried up to form a parapet and conceal the sloping slate roofs much loved by the later Victorians. The overall effect is one of calm composure achieved with simple means. The park in the centre is shared by the householders and from 1874 to 1896 was the home of Fitzwilliam Lawn Tennis Club. Lawn tennis is still played in the square but sadly not in the club.

THE CHURCH OF MOUNT CARMEL, FIRHOUSE

In the early 1970s, I was invited by the late Archbishop Ryan to serve on the jury of a competition for the design of a number of parish churches. The brief was not site-specific so that the designs could be adapted to any of the new suburban parishes. The aim of the competition was to produce about a dozen designs for low-cost parish churches.

The outstanding submission was by John Meagher, who, with his partner Shane de Blacam, built this church at Firhouse. The idea presented to the competition was simple; a church in a walled garden. The courtyard theme may have been inspired by the Court of Oranges in Cordoba and the exterior owes something to the work of the Dutch architect van Eyck, but the application was original and altogether appropriate.

The cruciform plan is placed in the centre and extends out to join the perimeter walls. The remaining garden is densely planted with trees, giving the effect of a tent with open sides set in an orchard clearing. There are views across the garden through the glass walls and the church is filled with dappled light and reflections of greenery.

Sadly, the parish proposes to abandon the existing design and with radical changes to the plan and the addition of a large pitched roof, all vestiges of the original concept will be removed.

THE IRISH MANAGEMENT INSTITUTE

This building reminds me of a view of Cetara on the Gulf of Salerno painted by John Robert Cozens in 1790. I wonder if the architect was inspired by a visit to the Mediterranean. The building is in fact in Sandyford, a few miles south of Dublin, and was designed by Arthur Gibney in the early 1970s. It is a seductive building which draws you gently in and reveals its attractions and complexities step by step. It is a striking image in which the building blocks are arranged irregularly in a staggered formation in response to the undulating topography of the site. The architect may have wanted to reduce both the scale of the building and the perceived importance of the Institute, and the effect is to bring to mind the friendly image and atmosphere of a Greek island village. The building appears to be cumulative yet each part is equally fresh in its sparkling whiteness. It has been carefully placed in the landscape as if by a Japanese gardener. This is a substantial achievement by a young architect confidently contributing to mainstream European architecture.

THE RESTAURANT BUILDING, UNIVERSITY COLLEGE DUBLIN

The restaurant building designed in 1973 by Robin Walker is distinguished from all the other buildings on the UCD campus by the fact that all of its external walled surfaces are made of glass. Other buildings have large areas of glass in one or other of their elevations which in many cases are then modified by means of grilles, permanent sunshades or brise-soleil, but in the restaurant the glass is there for all to see through. Remarkably, the glass is repeated on the building's north, south, east and west façades and the problems of glare and solar gain are acknowledged if not solved by the large oversailing of the roof.

In fact the building is conceived as a large square roof supported around its perimeter on eight columns. Between the ground and the roof, a number of irregularly shaped platforms are constructed to serve as intermediate floors and mezzanines. The whole is then enclosed in a series of vertical glass plates which extend from the edge of the floor to the slab above. The overall effect is one of transparency. Whereas the functions of most of the other buildings relate to introspection – reading, thinking, teaching - the restaurant is a social building that provides views over the extensive campus and the sea beyond. The building has many Miesian details – the square plan, the large expanse of glass, the L-shaped corner columns – but it also has personal idiosyncrasies which enliven the spatial experience and enrich the campus.

ST STEPHEN'S CHAPLAINCY, BELFIELD

Very often the preparation of the brief for a building can be a creative experience, as was the case here when Father Con Dowling, the other chaplains and myself struggled for almost a year defining the needs of the centre, which I designed in 1981.

St Stephen's serves as a home for the five residential chaplains and as a meeting place for students. Its design is based on the model of a nineteenth-century country house where generous reception rooms were available to the household and were planned with frequent large-scale entertainment in mind. Here the double-height entrance hall and the drawing room beyond occupy the centre of the plan. The services, which in the eighteenth-century house were located in the basement, are accommodated in two intermediate floors at either end of the building. The residential accommodation is on the upper floors with a two-storey-high living-room overlooked by the bedrooms on a mezzanine. As this was a small building adjacent to large neighbours, the problem of scale was important. A white textured concrete block was used which is in the same proportion to the building as the larger concrete panels are to the nearby School of Engineering.

An unusual feature of the building is the contemplation room, a circular space with lead-lined walls and doors leading to an enclosed courtyard. Here staff and students are encouraged to pause in their daily activities and meditate in the silence of the space.

THE ARK, TEMPLE BAR

The Ark, part of the Temple Bar redevelopment, is a children's theatre designed by Shane O'Toole and Michael Kelly. It occupies the site of the old Presbyterian Meeting House and extends from Eustace Street back to the new Meeting House Square.

It is hard to explain the attraction of this façade except that for me it has some consonance with the set of a Punch and Judy show. It expresses very accurately the complex and successful interior planning which placed the compact semi-circular auditorium behind the large folding door. When opened, the stage can be used simultaneously for indoor and outdoor audiences. The four brick boxes on the top represent four bays of a studio which is top lit and can be sub-divided into self-contained rooms. The window of the administrator's office on the top right corner of the building seems to be a defiant gesture to upset the symmetry. Otherwise the composition is very controlled; it is built up around the centre feature of the stylish stage curtain and the well detailed proscenium arch. I hope The Ark will open its stage to the public more often so that the façade will become animated with live performances.

DUBLIN CASTLE

The upper yard in Dublin Castle is a good example of a successful composition involving a variety of buildings from different periods with different functions, scales and materials. The buildings date from the eighteenth century and were built more or less on the foundations of the original thirteenth-century castle. It is not known for certain who the architects were but the overall effect is surprisingly cohesive. The impression of a barracks square is relieved by the projecting stone façades of the State Apartments and the Castle Hall opposite. In 1907, on the eve of a visit of King Edward to Dublin, the Irish Crown Jewels were stolen, reputedly by a civil servant who lived at No. 7 St James Terrace in Clonskeagh. Some years ago I moved to No. 6 St James Terrace and my neighbour suggested that I should dig extensively in my garden as he had done in his, to no avail.

It was in this courtyard that the Commanding Officer in the British Army handed over power to his counterpart in the Free State Army on 16 January 1922.

THE BULL WALL AND SOUTH WALL

Entry from Dublin Bay to the inner bay and the River Liffey is marked by the Poolbeg lighthouse and the North Bull lighthouse which stand 250 metres apart. The piers and the lighthouses were built during the eighteenth and early nineteenth century. Today the two exhilarating promenades stretch several kilometres into the bay.

To the inexperienced, Dublin Bay provides a safe and sheltered entry to the port through the narrow portals of the two lighthouses. But the bay has shallows and sandbanks and a narrow channel, and with a four-metre tide and a flowing river the navigation can be difficult. I experienced such difficulty late one summer's evening while returning in the fading light with friends from a regatta in Howth. As we approached the entrance in a small sailing boat, the tide turned and began to ebb, the wind dropped and without an engine the boat slipped sideways and began drifting slowly in the flow of the river. Suddenly we saw what appeared to be a very large tanker bearing down on us. We could see its masthead lights and two men walking briskly on the deck. We shouted 'Ahoy', banged the gunwales and splashed the water, but to no avail. We were at the point of abandoning the boat when we realised that the large black silhouette was in fact that of the Bull Wall and the boat drifting sideways caused the illusion that we were being run down by a tanker.

GANDON'S GRAVE

Drumcondra was our nearest social centre during our early teens. Every Saturday afternoon we went to the cinema known as the 'Drummer' and on Sunday afternoon we followed 'Drums', the local soccer team. Our outward journey was prompt and purposeful but we returned home by devious routes, exploring every byway and re-enacting scenes from the films or the match. In this way we came to know the small church and cemetery of St John The Baptist behind the Cat & Cage pub in the backwater that is Church Road. I did not discover until I was a student that the architect James Gandon (1742-1812) was buried there, as it were, in our midst.

Gandon was the most influential architect ever to practise in Ireland and with his two masterpieces, the Custom House and the Four Courts, he established a standard of architecture for Dublin which will serve it for all time. It is for this reason that in my annual address to the incoming students I spoke of Gandon and his work and urged everyone to make a pilgrimage to his grave. He was by all accounts a modest man. He spent his retirement years in his house in Lucan drawing and designing projects, which remain unbuilt, and died there in his eightieth year.

The grave is close to the south wall of the church in the shade of an old yew tree. The modest gravestone is a slab of limestone supported on four blocks of granite. A fifth support under the centre of the slab seems to have been added later.

The inscription is set out overleaf.

To the Memory of Captain Grose

F.R.S.

Who whilst in cheerful conversation

With his Friends

Expired in their Arms

Without a Sigh

18th of May

1791

Aged 60

Also his Friend

James Gandon

Architect

Born 1742 died 1821

INDEX OF SUBJECTS